Chadwick Public Library

Sexual Harassment

"This Doesn't Feel Right!"

by Kate Havelin

Consultant:
Sue Sattel
Chair, Sexual Harassment Task Force
National Coalition for Sex Equality in Education (NCSEE)

Perspectives on Relationships

LifeMatters
an imprint of Capstone Press
Mankato, Minnesota

LifeMatters books are published by Capstone Press
818 North Willow Street • Mankato, Minnesota 56001
http://www.capstone-press.com

Printed in the United States of America

Library of Congress Cataloging-in-Publication Data

Havelin, Kate, 1961–
      Sexual harassment: "this doesn't feel right!" / by Kate Havelin.
          p.   cm. — (Perspectives on relationships)
      Includes bibliographical references and index.
      Summary: Describes sexual harassment, its possible causes, its effects, and what can be done to stop it.
      ISBN 0-7368-0289-4 (book). ISBN 0-7368-0295-9 (series)
      1. Sexual harassment of women—Juvenile literature. 2. Sexual harassment—Juvenile literature. [1. Sexual harassment.]
      I. Title. II. Series.
      HQ1237.H39   2000
      305—dc21   99-31197
                                         CIP

Staff Credits

Anne Heller, Kristin Thoennes, editors; Adam Lazar, designer; Heidi Schoof, photo researcher

Photo Credits

Cover: Index Stock Photography/©Jenssen
CNP/Archive Photos/16
FPG International/©Jill Sabella, 7; ©Arthur Tilley, 41; ©Ron Chapple, 59
International Stock/©Scott Barrow, 15, 21; ©Bob Firth, 55
Photri, Inc./©Jeff Greenberg, 33; ©Bachmann, 35
REUTERS/Archive Photos/ 24; ©Steve Marcus, 28; ©Bruce Young, 45
The Picture Cube, Inc./©Jeff Greenberg, 51
Unicorn Stock Photos/©H. H. Thomas, 19
Uniphoto, Inc./11, 26, 37, 49

A 0 9 8 7 6 5 4 3 2 1

Table of Contents

Chapter Overview

Sexual harassment includes any unwanted sexual words or conduct.

Sexual harassment is against the law.

Flirting and sexual harassment are different. Flirting is usually acceptable behavior between two people. Sexual harassment is unwanted, one-way behavior.

Males and females can both be sexually harassed and cause sexual harassment.

People who are sexually harassed may feel bad, ashamed, or defenseless. Repeated sexual harassment can cause some people to lose self-confidence. Stress from sexual harassment causes some victims to become physically sick.

Chapter 1

What Is Sexual Harassment?

What Sexual Harassment Is

Sexual harassment is any unwanted sexual attention, actions, or words. The key word is *unwanted.* That means the words or actions are not welcome.

Sexual harassment includes a range of conduct. It includes everything from rude comments from a stranger to being forced to have sex with someone. Some incidents of sexual harassment are simply annoying. Other cases, however, are serious and deeply hurt victims and others.

Myth: Sexual harassment goes away if you ignore it.

Fact: Harassers often continue to bother their victims. They repeatedly make sexual comments to, stare at, or grab their victims. The offensive behavior may continue for days, weeks, or even years if nothing is done to stop it.

Harassment includes many kinds of improper behavior. Here are some behaviors that are considered sexual harassment:

Unnecessary and unwelcome physical contact such as touching, patting, pinching, or kissing

Sexual assault

Jokes, comments, indirect suggestions, or taunting about a person's body, clothes, age, or marital status

Continually asking a person for a date after he or she has repeatedly said no

Pressuring a person to have sex

Asking a person about his or her sexual fantasies, preferences, or sex life

Sexual looks or gestures such as licking the lips or wiggling the tongue

Sexual pictures or words displayed on a public surface

Stalking, or continually following, a person

Sexual Harassment

What Sexual Harassment Is Not

Sexual harassment is not the same as flirting, joking, or dating. It is okay to flirt with people you like. Usually flirting is mutual between two people. Jokes are a natural thing among friends. Sexual harassment, however, crosses the line between what is and is not okay.

The chart shows how some teens sorted out the differences between flirting and harassment.

Flirting	Harassment
Feels good	Feels bad
Makes me feel attractive	Makes me feel cheap
Is a compliment	Is degrading
Is two-way	Is one-way
Is positive	Feels out-of-control
I like it	Makes me feel helpless

Dana is saving money for college. **Dana Gets Asked Out** Every day she rushes from school to her waitress job at a nearby restaurant. Today her friend Ben walked her to work. Dana likes Ben, so she was thrilled when he asked her for a date on Friday.

Dana smiles as she walks into work, thinking about Ben. Her manager, Mr. Edwards, corners her in the kitchen. He puts his arm around Dana's shoulders, "Hey, sweetie," he says, "Why the big smile? I bet I can guess what's on your mind. I bet a pretty girl like you would appreciate a real man. How about you and me getting together tonight after your shift?"

Dana feels sick. She does not want Mr. Edwards to touch her. She does not want him to ask her out. She wants to yell at him but she feels scared. Luckily, an older waitress named Alice walks in. She clears her throat loudly and tells Mr. Edwards there's a problem in the dining room. Mr. Edwards lets go of Dana and glares at Alice as he walks out. Alice warns Dana to keep an eye out for Mr. Edwards. "He tries to put the moves on all the young girls," Alice says.

Dana wants to cry. She just wants to do her job and not have to think about being hassled. All Dana can think about through her shift is how to stay away from Mr. Edwards. He scares her a little. She does not know how to make him stop. She worries that Mr. Edwards will get mad if she says no. She doesn't want to lose this job, but she also doesn't like her manager's behavior.

The women's liberation movement in the 1970s pushed lawmakers and judges to enforce the laws against sexual harassment. By 1980, the government ruled that sexual harassment was a form of sexual discrimination and was illegal.

Sexual Harassment Is Illegal

Sexual harassment is against the law. Title IX of the Education Amendments of 1972 outlawed sexual harassment. However, it took years for courts to enforce the law. Now many schools and businesses have policies to prevent sexual harassment. The courts continue to decide sexual harassment cases. Still, some people do not understand what sexual harassment is or that they are being sexually harassed.

All Kinds of People Are Sexually Harassed

Sexual harassment can happen to anyone. It affects girls and women as well as boys and men. It happens to people who are pretty and people who are plain. It can happen to people who are young or old, rich or poor. In addition, all kinds of people can sexually harass others. Although men are most likely to harass women, sometimes women or girls do the harassing.

Courts have even ruled that sexual harassment has happened between people of the same gender. That means males sexually harass males, and females sexually harass females. Some people are sexually harassed because they are gay or lesbian, or attracted to people of the same sex. However, a person's sexual attractions do not explain or excuse any sexual harassment.

One 1993 New York case of sexual harassment happened in a swimming pool. It involved a game called whirlpooling. Boys would surround a girl in a pool and try to remove her bathing suit. The boys groped some girls and assaulted others. Police arrested seven boys.

Where Does Sexual Harassment Happen?

Sexual harassment can happen anywhere. Many times sexual harassment occurs at work or school. It happens at home when victims receive offensive phone calls. Sometimes people receive repeated calls from an unknown caller who quickly hangs up. Sexual harassment can happen on the school bus or in public places.

How Does Sexual Harassment Make a Person Feel?

Sexual harassment often makes a person feel uncomfortable, tense, scared, or mad. Repeated harassment can hurt a person's self-image. A person may begin to doubt his or her worth. People who have been harassed may feel less confident. However, people who report harassment or take action to stop it often feel better.

Some people who face continued harassment become physically sick. Some get frequent headaches. Others lose their appetite or cannot sleep. Some get an upset stomach or frequent infections. The mental stress affects their body as well as their mind.

Courtney takes a city bus home from her high school. **Courtney Makes a Decision** Today the bus is full and she has to stand. A man gets on after her and stands next to her. Suddenly Courtney feels his hand on her leg. She glares at him but he just smiles. Courtney's face turns red. She does not want to make a scene. She does not want everyone on the bus to know he is touching her.

Finally, Courtney decides to say something. Just as she is ready to ask the man to move his hand, the bus stops and he gets off. The man waves to her as he saunters off. Courtney feels angry. She wishes she had said something to him. Courtney promises herself that another time she will say something right away. She won't let someone else control the situation.

Points to Consider

Have you ever been the victim of sexual harassment? How did it feel?

Have you ever sexually harassed another person? How do you think the other person felt?

How would you react if a manager or a teacher treated you like Mr. Edwards treated Dana?

Chapter Overview

Many cases of sexual harassment are based on a power struggle. One person wants to prove his or her power over another person.

Some cases of sexual harassment occur because of unfair gender differences. Males and females often are treated differently. Men traditionally have had more power. Some men resent women who expect to be treated equally.

Females face greater risk of being raped than males do. That may explain why girls and women consider more incidents to be sexual harassment than males do.

Some sexual harassment occurs because people don't understand that their behavior is harassing.

Chapter 2

Why Sexual Harassment Happens

Sexual harassment happens for many different reasons. Some harassers purposely bother people. Other harassers do not intend to make people feel bad. Those harassers may not understand that their words or actions cause pain. No one can say for certain why all cases of sexual harassment occur. However, many incidents of sexual harassment have some common causes. This chapter describes four of those causes. As you read, think about why you think harassment happens.

A major poll of high school students showed many reasons why kids sexually harass each other. Students said they harassed because:

Everyone does it.

They thought the person liked it.

They wanted to date the person they harassed.

Friends egged them on.

They wanted something from the person they harassed.

They wanted the person they harassed to view them as having power.

Maritza Is Angry

Maritza used to have a crush on Brian. One day she asked him out. He laughed, thinking she was joking. Now Maritza is angry with Brian. She wants to hurt him, so she spreads gossip about him.

Soon other people tease Brian. He does not know why other students whisper about him and laugh when they see him. A friend tells Brian about Maritza's cruel rumors. Brian is stunned, hurt, and a little scared. He does not know how to stop Maritza's lies.

Finally, Brian confronts Maritza. She sneers at him and tells him that she wants to make his life miserable. She wants Brian to be afraid of her power. Soon, kids begin to realize Maritza is out of control. Even though Brian's friends stand by him, he feels burned. It takes him a long time to trust a girl again.

Power

There are many ways to have power. Some people have power because of their age, job, or personality. For example, teachers have power over students because of their job. Some adults have power because of their age and authority. Parents have power over their children. A few kids may influence what other kids do, say, or wear. That influence is a kind of power.

Some people use their power to hurt other people. For example, a popular basketball player might tease another student about his clothes, his weight, or his clumsiness. If more kids follow the player's lead, life may become miserable for the other student.

Not all power struggles are related to sexual harassment. The example of the basketball player is not a case of sexual harassment. However, sexual harassment often is mainly about power. For example, some bosses have threatened to dismiss female employees if they don't grant sexual favors. Stalkers have power when they frighten their victims. People who make forceful sexual advances use power over others.

Different Treatment of the Sexes

Men historically have had more power than women have. Men have controlled governments and made laws. They have not allowed women to work, vote, own property, or go to school. Today, however, both Canadian and American laws give men and women equal rights.

Despite the laws, men and women still are not always treated equally. Many people still view females as the "weaker" sex. Women often earn far less than men do. Men have most of the public power. For example, men control nearly all of the 100 seats in the U.S. Senate. Male professional athletes receive more attention and money than female athletes do.

That unequal treatment can lead to sexual harassment. Many men resent women who move into what traditionally were men's areas. For example, Sandra Huffman worked on a loading dock for Pepsi-Cola in Minnesota. She endured continued sexual harassment from male coworkers. The men told Huffman that women did not belong on a loading dock. A jury awarded Huffman $530,000 for the pain of being sexually harassed.

A bunch of friends from **Two Views of One Incident** both the boys and the girls' swim team get together after meets for a snack. After the last meet, the boys decided to play a trick on the girls. The boys stood outside the girls' locker room. As the girls came out, the boys grabbed and blindfolded them. The girls kicked and screamed. Ms. Henson, the swim coach, came out to see what was going on.

The boys explained it was a joke and that they didn't mean to hurt anyone. It was supposed to be funny, but the girls were angry. They didn't think being grabbed and blindfolded was funny. The boys apologized but didn't understand why the girls reacted so strongly.

When both teams still seemed angry with each other a week later, Ms. Henson called a meeting. The girls explained that they felt scared because they couldn't see who was grabbing them. They felt like someone was trying to hurt or even rape them. The boys repeated that they were just joking. Some said the girls couldn't take a joke. The boys said they would never hurt their friends.

Ms. Henson concluded that the boys needed to think more about their actions first. She explained that it is not okay to grab and blindfold people. The boys agreed they probably would not like being grabbed and blindfolded. Both teams agreed it helped to talk about what happened.

Sexual stereotypes, or overly simple opinions, often show differences between males and females. Here are some sexual stereotypes that often are not true.

Girls cry easily.	Boys don't cry.
Girls can't take a joke.	Boys will be boys.
Girls who have sex are sluts.	Boys who have sex are studs.

Differences Between the Sexes

Males and females are equal but not the same. For example, basic physical differences between the sexes may explain why the genders often see sexual harassment differently. Men are generally bigger and stronger than women are. Women face greater risk of being raped or sexually assaulted than men do. Consequently, women fear rape much more than men do.

Women who fear rape may be more likely to feel threatened by a man's words or actions. Females may not consciously worry about rape. However, rape happens to at least one in seven females. As a result, it is a legitimate concern for women. Therefore, it makes sense that girls and women may feel threatened by things that don't upset males.

Physical differences also may influence how the genders relate to one another. For example, getting their menstrual period is a sign for girls that they are becoming women. Boys don't have one distinct sign like menstruation to show they are becoming men. One expert believes that boys view having sex as proof that they have become men.

Many boys and girls say they feel pressured to have sex. The pressure, however, usually comes in different ways. Girls get pressure from their boyfriends to have sex. By contrast, many boys feel pressure from other boys to have sex. Male buddies often tease each other about how much or how little sex they have. That male pressure may cause boys to push girls too hard to have sex. This pushing can become harassment.

Males and females often view sex differently. Many boys and men talk about sex as "scoring." Many girls and women view sex as an expression of love. That difference in how the genders view sex also may explain why they often view sexual harassment differently.

"Everybody wants to know if you've scored or not. There's just a lot of pressure to have sex with a girl."
—Ralph, age 16

Lack of Knowledge

Sometimes teens and even some adults don't know how to approach someone romantically. It is not always easy to talk with a person you like. Sometimes the more you like someone, the more embarrassed or tongue-tied you become.

Some people may try to make sexual jokes with a person they have a crush on. The jokes offend that person, who doesn't understand that the individual doesn't know what to do or say. Misunderstandings between two people often result when one person has trouble expressing his or her feelings. These misunderstandings are sometimes viewed as sexual harassment.

Points to Consider

Why do you think sexual harassment happens?

How would you feel if a person with more power such as a manager or a teacher asked you out? Would you feel differently if a fellow student or teen used the same words to ask you out? Why might the two situations make you feel differently?

What ways can you think of in which males and females are treated differently?

Think of one stereotype about males and one about females. Do you think they are true? Explain.

Chapter Overview

Some true examples show how widespread sexual harassment is and that it affects all kinds of people.

The people in these cases have shaped society's views of what harassment is.

Courts have acted to stop sexual harassment in cases such as these.

Chapter 3

Real-Life Stories of Sexual Harassment

Unfortunately, sexual harassment has happened often. The famous cases described in this chapter broke new legal ground. They also may have expanded or changed how we view sexual harassment.

Anita Hill and Clarence Thomas

One famous case of alleged sexual harassment happened in 1993. That is when Judge Clarence Thomas was nominated to the U.S. Supreme Court. One of his former employees, Anita Hill, said that Thomas had sexually harassed her. They had worked at the Equal Employment Opportunity Office, a government office created to fight harassment.

Anita Hill testified that Clarence Thomas joked about porn movies and made other offensive remarks. Hill said she did not report the harassment because she feared it would hurt her career.

Thomas denied he ever harassed Hill. He said he had never even asked her out. Many men questioned whether she was telling the truth. Many women rallied around Hill, buying buttons and bumper stickers that said, "I Believe Anita."

Clarence Thomas won a close vote that allowed him to become a Supreme Court Justice.

This case is important because it focused attention on sexual harassment. Anita Hill's story made many other women step forward with their own incidents of harassment. The U.S. government reported a 70 percent increase in sexual harassment cases in the first three months after Hill's testimony. Her testimony also angered many people. The case revealed a huge gender gap. Many women said, "Men don't get it." Many men shook their head and wondered why women were so upset.

Spur Posse

One of the most dramatic cases of alleged sexual harassment among teens happened in California in 1993. The story involved a group of Lakewood High School male athletes and their friends. The group called themselves the Spur Posse. Sheriff's deputies arrested nine members of the group for alleged sex crimes. The 15- to 18-year-old boys were charged with having sex with girls as young as 10. It was supposed to be part of the Spur Posse's competition to see which boy could have the most sex.

The boys said the girls had not been forced to have sex and were willing. Within a week, all but one of the boys was released. One 16-year-old was found guilty of indecent conduct with a 10-year-old girl. The Spur Posse story sparked widespread attention. Some of the boys' parents said they were proud of their boys for having sex. The boys were considered "studs." However, the girls who had sex with Spur Posse boys got a different reputation. Many of their classmates considered the girls who had sex to be "sluts."

This case is important because it shows how completely different some people view sex for girls and boys.

Jake Baker's On-Line Fantasies

A University of Michigan student named Abraham Jacob Alkhabaz wrote some sexual fantasies. He posted them on the Internet using the name Jake Baker. Several of Baker's stories describe raping, torturing, and killing girls or women. He also e-mailed a man several times about kidnapping, raping, and murdering a woman.

Baker named one story after a classmate of his. He never contacted the woman. Instead, a girl in Moscow who read his story told her father. Eventually the story got back to officials at Baker's school. University officials suspended Baker in 1995, less than two weeks after they learned of his on-line stories. The school said Baker posed a threat to the woman. "Jane Doe," as the woman is known in court papers, says she feels threatened by Baker.

The Federal Bureau of Investigation (FBI) arrested Baker. He was charged with breaking federal laws for transmitting his stories and e-mails. Since then, his case has gone before several judges and is still not resolved.

This case is important because it shows the power of words. Baker never physically harassed "Jane Doe." This case may influence free speech on the Internet.

Student-to-Student Sexual Harassment

LaShonda Davis's classmate sexually harassed her repeatedly in a Georgia elementary school. The boy tried to touch her breasts and genital area and made dirty statements. He behaved in a sexually suggestive manner. LaShonda reported the harassment to her teachers each time it happened. Her mother talked with the school principal each time. The boy also harassed other girls. With LaShonda, the girls tried to talk with the principal. Over the five months that LaShonda was harassed, the principal did little to discipline the boy. LaShonda's grades dropped, and her father found a suicide note that she had written.

After five months of harassing LaShonda, the boy pleaded guilty to charges of sexual assault. LaShonda's mother filed a lawsuit that went all the way to the U.S. Supreme Court. In 1999, the court ruled that public schools can be sued for failing to stop sexual harassment by students. Public school districts that receive federal funds can be liable when they are deliberately indifferent to harassment of one student by another.

This case is important because it could lead to widespread sexual harassment training among educators in public schools. Public schools may have to pay damages if they fail to stop a student from sexually harassing another student.

Tailhook: The Navy's Shame

An example of widespread harassment happened in Las Vegas in 1991. More than 5,000 current and former Navy aircraft carrier pilots attended the annual Tailhook Association symposium. Only 4 percent were women.

Lt. Paula Coughlin and at least 82 other women endured the harassment. They were forced to pass a double-file line of two dozen male pilots. Many of the men had been drinking. They grabbed the women's breasts, buttocks, and other body parts. Some of the women feared they would be gang-raped.

When the women reported the assault, the Navy did nothing. As the scandal received more attention, the Secretary of the Navy was forced to resign. However, no pilots faced lawsuits. Lt. Coughlin said pilots who resented her publicizing the attack continued to harass her. She resigned from the Navy in 1994.

This case is important because it shows how widespread sexual harassment can be. The final report on Tailhook found that 83 women were assaulted. The incident shows how hard it can be to overcome harassment. Sometimes people who report harassment end up being further harassed. Lt. Coughlin said she suffered a great deal of retaliation, or revenge, for coming forward.

Points to Consider

Why do you think men and women responded so differently to the Hill-Thomas case?

Do you think a Spur Posse case could happen in your school? Why or why not?

How would you react if you learned some kids were competing to see who could have the most sex?

What would you think if a younger brother or sister were sexually harassed in elementary school?

Why do you think Lt. Paula Coughlin resigned from the Navy?

Chapter Overview

Sexual harassment in schools is a serious problem that affects both males and females.

Most sexual harassment in schools happens between students.

Sometimes teachers or other adults in schools harass students.

Sexual harassment can make students dislike or even quit school. It can make students feel nervous, afraid, or angry.

Chapter 4

Sexual Harassment at School

BRINNGGG. The bell rings and Rosa rushes out of history class.

Rosa Gets Detention

She wants to get to her locker before Tom and his friends get there. Lately, Tom has been hassling Rosa. He stands too close and stares at her. She turns down the hallway toward her locker and sees Tom and his friends standing in front of her locker. Rosa wants to cry. She is afraid to go to her locker. She is afraid Tom will grab her the way he did yesterday. Instead, she ducks into the girls' bathroom. She stays there until the bell rings. Then she dashes to her locker and races to English class—late again.

Mrs. Smithson looks up when Rosa walks in. She asks Rosa to come to her desk and hands her a tardy slip. She tells Rosa, "Take this down to the principal's office. You will have detention today for being late." Rosa takes the slip of paper, walks out of class, and feels defeated.

Most cases of school harassment occur in the classroom. Hallways are a close second for where most harassment happens.

Many young people face sexual harassment at school. It can happen from elementary school through college. It happens in private and public schools. Sexual harassment can hurt both girls and boys. However, girls are three times more likely to be harassed than boys are. Also, boys are much more likely to be harassers than girls are.

Studies show that most school harassment cases occur between students. In a few cases, however, teachers or other school staff are the harassers. Two major studies found that more than three-quarters of the young people polled had been harassed at school.

The American Association of University Women (AAUW) polled 1,632 students in grades 8 through 11. The AAUW's "Hostile Hallways" report found that:

81 percent of all students polled said they had been sexually harassed at school

85 percent of girls had been harassed

76 percent of boys had been harassed

The "Hostile Hallways" report showed that students:

Were touched, grabbed, pinched, or intentionally brushed up against in a sexual way

Were flashed or mooned

Had sexual rumors spread about them

Had their clothing removed or pulled at in a sexual way

Were shown, given, or left sexual pictures or notes

Had sexual graffiti written about them on lockers, bathroom walls, or other places

Were forced to kiss someone or do something sexual

Were called lesbian or gay

Were spied on while dressing or showering

Quote

"If you can't feel comfortable at school, how can you get a good education? Something has got to change."—14-year-old Illinois girl

"Being sexually harassed at school made me feel upset, angry, and violated. I mean, I shouldn't have to take this crap at school, should I? It's my right to go to school and not be harassed, isn't it? I feel confused because I wonder if all guys think those things about me! I feel insecure after this happens. I hate it. I shouldn't have to feel sexually intimidated by people who barely know me."—15-year-old Vermont girl

The Wellesley Center for Research on Women polled 4,200 girls in a *Seventeen* magazine survey. The Wellesley survey results showed that:

97 percent were harassed by boys

89 percent received unwanted sexual comments, gestures, or looks

83 percent were pinched, touched, or grabbed in a sexually harassing way at school

10 percent were forced to do something sexual

39 percent were harassed daily during the past year

76 percent of girls told at least one person about being harassed in school

45 percent of the time nothing happened to the harasser, even when girls told a teacher or administrator

4 percent were harassed by teachers, administrators, or other school staff

Nicki loves music and wants to be a musician. Lately, however, band **Nicki Dreads Band** practice has been stressful. Mr. Sherman, the band teacher, makes Nicki nervous. He stands close to her and sometimes rubs her back. One day she thought he was looking down her shirt.

Nicki is not sure if she is imagining things. Maybe Mr. Sherman was not trying to look at her breasts. Nicki felt sick the day Mr. Sherman asked her to stay after class to work on a new piece of music. First, he had her run through the music. Then he casually put his arm around her and tried to hug her when she finished playing. Nicki pulled away, quickly grabbed her books, and told Mr. Sherman she had to go.

Nicki does not want to face Mr. Sherman alone again. She thinks about quitting band. However, she doesn't know how to explain that to her friends or parents. Finally, Nicki tells her friend Gina. Nicki learns that other students also have complained about Mr. Sherman. Nicki and Gina decide to talk with their counselor.

 Did You Know?

A Georgia high school student named Christine Franklin was forced to have sex with a teacher. She used to help grade papers for teacher and coach Andrew Hill. Franklin said Hill asked about her sex life and eventually got her to have sex with him. Franklin took her case to the U.S. Supreme Court. The justices ruled that students like Franklin who are sexually harassed can sue schools for damages. Until then, victims of sexual harassment could only sue for lost wages.

That Supreme Court ruling in 1992 opened the door for many other students who are harassed. They can go to court and make a school pay for their suffering. Schools are supposed to provide students a safe place to learn that is free of harassment. States like California and Minnesota require schools to have sexual harassment policies.

Teacher-Student Harassment

Most young people feel uncomfortable when teachers or other school staff harass them. A student may skip that teacher's class or quit that coach's team because of the unwanted attention. Adults who sexually harass students break the trust young people should have in their school staff.

Some teachers physically harass students. They touch students in a sexual way. Some have what they consider "love affairs" with students. However, any kind of a sexual relationship between a student and a teacher can be considered sexual harassment.

Teachers are in a position of power over their students. Often students may be afraid of getting bad grades if they shun a teacher's sexual advances. It is wrong for a teacher to use his or her power to harass a student in any way.

Points to Consider

Do the types of things listed in the "Hostile Hallways" report happen in your school? If so, what has your school done about it?

Have you ever been harassed in school? If so, how did you handle it?

Who would you go to if a teacher or other school staff person harassed you?

Does your school have a sexual harassment policy? If so, what does it say? If not, what would you like it to say?

Chapter Overview

Teens sometimes face sexual harassment at work.

Some cases of sexual harassment at work are not clear-cut. It may be hard to know if sexual harassment actually occurred. It is important for teens to learn to trust their instincts.

Canadian and U.S. laws require employers to provide a workplace free of sexual harassment. Courts hear many cases of harassment on the job.

Many businesses have written policies concerning sexual harassment. Employees can review those policies to learn how to handle harassment.

Chapter 5

Sexual Harassment at Work

Some bosses, coworkers, or customers harass people on the job. Sexual harassment in the workplace is wrong, no matter who the harasser is. The law requires employers to provide a workplace free from sexual harassment.

On-the-job sexual harassment usually makes a person feel bad. A Working Women's Institute study found that 96 percent of women who were sexually harassed felt stressed. More than a third of the women reported the stress interfered with their ability to work.

Workplace harassment can affect more than just adults with full-time careers. On-the-job harassment also can affect teens who have jobs. Unfortunately, sexual harassment happens in many workplaces.

Some Sexual Harassment Is Not Clear-Cut

Sometimes sexual harassment isn't clear-cut. For example, a young person may not be sure whether the boss is being helpful or pushy. Here are some tips for handling situations in which sexual harassment may not be clear-cut.

Listen to your instincts.

Sometimes you may feel uneasy without knowing exactly why. That uneasiness may be a signal that something is wrong. It's important to trust your instincts. Try to figure out what is causing the discomfort. Does a coworker stand too close to you? Is your manager overly friendly? Do you tense up every time a certain customer comes in? What does that customer do to make you tense?

Talk with someone you trust.

It often helps to talk through a problem with a friend. Is there another trusted person at work with whom you could talk? It's important to choose someone who you trust will not spread rumors or repeat your conversation. You might tell your concerns to a friend and get his or her reaction. Perhaps your school counselor can help.

Try to change the situation.

Often you can do something to improve the situation before it gets worse. You may be able to resolve the issue without quitting or suffering silently. For example, are you nervous riding home alone with a certain man after you baby-sit his kids? Perhaps you could ask to bring a friend along when you baby-sit for that family. That way you will not be alone with the man in the car.

Dave's Too-Friendly Neighbor

Dave mows several neighbors' lawns in the morning each week when most customers are at work. However, Mrs. Andrews is at home. She often invites Dave in for a glass of lemonade. The cool drink tastes great, but the conversation makes Dave nervous.

Mrs. Andrews constantly asks Dave if he has a girlfriend. She always comments on how good-looking Dave is and how strong his arms are. Dave thinks Mrs. Andrews is flirting, but he's not sure. He feels uneasy.

One week Mrs. Andrews sat on her deck sunbathing while Dave mowed the lawn. She asked Dave to put sunscreen on her back. He didn't want to, but he didn't know what to say. Mrs. Andrews tried to grab his hand, but Dave pulled away and quickly finished the lawn.

The next week Dave asked a friend to mow Mrs. Andrews' lawn. The boys decided to team up. Now each boy brings a lawn mower, and they mow lawns twice as fast.

A 1992 Working Women report estimated that sexual harassment claims costs Fortune 500 businesses $6.7 million a year. The costs come from absenteeism, staff turnover, and reduced productivity.

The History of Workplace Harassment

Harassment on the job isn't new. Female factory workers complained about being harassed almost 100 years ago. Until the 1980s, no laws were enforced against sexual harassment in the workplace. In the 1980s, both the U.S. and Canadian governments ruled that sexual harassment at work is illegal.

Since the laws were passed, the courts have handled many workplace sexual harassment cases. In general, courts rule on two kinds of sexual harassment—quid pro quo and hostile environment.

The Latin phrase *quid pro quo* means "this for that." When it comes to sexual harassment cases, it often means "sex for jobs." For example, a boss may pressure his employee to have sex with him to keep her job.

A hostile environment includes any comments, actions, or behaviors that create an unpleasant or abusive atmosphere. For example, coworkers who display pictures of naked people may create a hostile work environment.

Federal laws limit how much money employees can collect from employers for sexual harassment. Damage awards can range from $50,000 to $300,000, depending on the company's size.

Sometimes a person faces both kinds of sexual harassment. Florida lifeguard Beth Ann Faragher did. Faragher said her direct supervisors created a sexually hostile environment. They touched Faragher and other female lifeguards and made off-color comments about women. One supervisor told Faragher, "Date me or clean toilets for a year." That comment is a clear example of quid pro quo. Faragher sued. The U.S. Supreme Court ruled in her favor in 1998.

Employers can be held legally responsible when an employee in a position of authority sexually harasses someone. That means that victims of harassment can sue employers for damages. However, victims should first try to resolve the problem using their company's grievance procedures. It's a good idea to talk with your supervisor or someone in human resources to learn your company's policies.

Company Policies Against Harassment

Many companies have written policies about sexual harassment. Businesses often have a process that allows employees to make formal complaints. The U.S. Equal Employment Opportunity Commission (EEOC) oversees workplaces with 15 or more employees. As a result, EEOC laws do not cover young people in independent jobs like lawn mowing or baby-sitting. However, many young people have retail or fast-food jobs, which the EEOC laws do cover.

According to a 1993 *New England Journal of Medicine* report, nearly 75 percent of female medical students said they had been sexually harassed.

Hold the Ketchup and the Comments

Glenda works the late shift at a fast-food restaurant. Some regular customers come in after the bars close. A few of the customers are drunk and make comments about Glenda. They tell her how well she fills out her uniform and ask what she is doing after work.

Glenda has learned to keep a wet rag in her hand. She uses it to splash customers "accidentally" when they get too close to her. Since she told her manager about the persistent rude comments, he has tried to schedule Tony to close with her. Tony and Glenda have swapped some duties. She switches to the kitchen when the noisy regulars arrive while Tony handles the counter.

Quitting or Losing a Job Because of Harassment

On-the-job harassment makes work unpleasant. Some employees decide they would rather quit than stay in a hostile workplace. For example, a 1998 Supreme Court case involved a salesperson named Kimberly Ellerth. She testified that one of her supervisors at Burlington Industries continually harassed her. She never told other managers about the harassment. Ellerth was promoted once and suffered no obvious punishment for refusing her supervisor's harassment. However, she felt she had to resign. The Supreme Court ruled Ellerth was harassed and could receive damages from her former employer.

Sometimes harassers end up losing their job because of their actions. Perhaps one of the best-known cases involved former U.S. Senator Bob Packwood. More than 20 former staff people said the senator harassed them. He resigned in 1993 because of the charges. Many people believe that Packwood's case shows how seriously sexual harassment in the workplace is now taken.

Groundbreakers Often Face Sexual Harassment

Sexual harassment occurs in all kinds of jobs. However, women who work in nontraditional careers often are more likely to be harassed. For example, studies show that female bankers and surgeons report high levels of sexual harassment. Men once dominated those professions. Some men resent women in careers that once only men had. It is believed that men in formerly all-female fields like nursing also face increased harassment.

Points to Consider

Have you ever been harassed on the job? If so, what happened and how did you handle it?

What would you do if a boss harassed you? Would you respond differently if the harasser were a coworker? a customer?

What do you think about female bankers and surgeons facing so much sexual harassment?

Chapter Overview

Sometimes the best way to stop a harasser is simply to ask the person to stop.

It often helps to talk with a friend or trusted adult about harassment.

It is important to keep track of harassment. Write down who did it, what was said or done, and when and where the harassment occurred.

Some victims choose to write their harasser a letter.

Other victims decide to file a complaint or lawsuit to stop the harassment.

Chapter 6

What to Do About Sexual Harassment

Sexual harassment seldom stops on its own. Ignoring harassment will not make it go away. In fact, only an estimated 5 percent of sexual harassment is reported. Often ignoring the problem makes victims continue to feel powerless.

Harassment includes a range of behaviors. Therefore, how harassment is handled depends on how serious it is. This chapter offers ideas on how to handle different kinds of harassment.

Seventy-five percent of the time, sexual harassment gets worse when it is ignored.

The Best Way to Stop Harassment: Tell the Harasser

Some experts believe that harassers stop 90 percent of the time when asked. Harassers need to hear that their words or actions are not acceptable. Here are some tips on how to handle harassers' rude comments and jokes.

Do not laugh. Your silence sends a strong message that the harasser's comment isn't funny.

Leave the room. Leaving makes it clear that you don't want to hear such comments. It keeps you from hearing offensive remarks.

Say something. Tell the harasser that you do not think the joke or comment is funny. Be firm but polite.

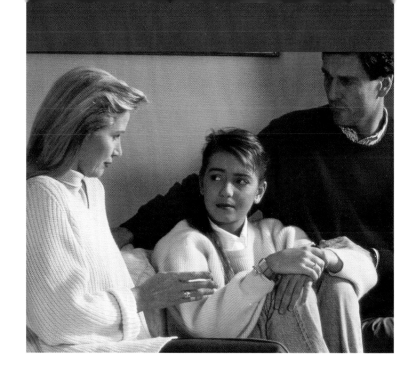

Telling harassers to stop works if you feel comfortable facing the harasser. Young people who are harassed by adults probably should not approach their harasser alone. Some people fear they may lose their job for reporting harassment. Others worry they will face increased anger from their harasser if they report the mistreatment. You can still work to stop harassment, even if you are not comfortable facing the harasser directly.

When You Cannot Confront the Harasser

There are several options available when you cannot confront the harasser directly.

1. Tell someone else.

Talking with a friend or someone you trust can help you see that you aren't alone. The person may have ideas for how to help you. You may feel better just having another person know what has happened. It may help prove that you were harassed if you must go to court.

You should keep any notes, gifts, or cartoons you have received from the harasser. They could be used as evidence.

2. Keep track of the harassment.

It is important to keep a record of what has happened. It helps to write down a few facts about each incident of sexual harassment soon after they happen. That helps you not to forget any important facts. A written record can help you prove to others that the sexual harassment happened. You need to record:

Who harassed you

What he or she said or did

When the harassment occurred

Where the harassment took place

Who else may have seen or heard the harassment

What happened when you reported the abuse to someone in charge

3. Write a letter.

Many people prefer writing the harasser rather than directly facing him or her. Writing a letter lets you say exactly what you want. When you write to a harasser:

Be clear and direct. It often helps to use *I* statements. For example: "I was angry when you pulled my bra strap in front of your friends."

Do not apologize for your feelings.

Be specific about comments or actions that you found to be harassing.

Be specific about what you want to happen. For example: "I do not want you to hang around my locker."

State your plan about what you will do if harassment continues. For example: "I will go to our supervisor if you continue to bother me at work."

Follow through with your plan. That means if the harassment continues, you need to report it.

Keep a copy of your letter as proof you tried to stop the harasser.

Jane is tired of the way Will is acting. She talked with her

Jane Writes a Letter

mother, who suggested writing Will a letter. Jane is nervous writing the letter, but she knows she needs to do something to stop Will.

October 7

Dear Will,

I am writing to tell you that I do not like the way you have treated me. I feel uncomfortable with your actions, which have included these instances:

September 2—You and your friends cornered me by my locker and would not let me pass. I could not get my math book and was late for class.

September 16—You pushed me into Ms. Jensen's empty classroom and grabbed my breasts.

September 21—You and Steve drew rude pictures of a naked person. You labeled the picture with my name and passed it around our science class.

Your behavior offends me. It is sexual harassment. I want you to stop harassing me immediately.

Do not block my locker. Do not grab me or touch me in any way. Do not draw pictures of me. If you continue to harass me, I will tell Mr. Martin, the assistant principal.

Sincerely,
Jane

4. Tell someone in authority.

Sometimes victims need someone in power to help stop the harassment. You may want to tell someone in authority about the harasser. A sympathetic teacher, coach, or counselor may be able to help. A manager or other supervisor at work may be able to stop the harassment. Your parents also may be able to help stop the harassment. A parent can go with you to meet with a principal or manager.

5. Be prepared for retaliation.

Some harassers continue their rude behavior even after they are told to stop. Some even become more offensive after victims speak out. Some victims face retaliation as harassers try to strike back and get revenge against their victims. It is important that you find people to support you if this happens. Friends can help you through a hard time. You may want to talk with others who have gone through harassment. Many women's organizations have counselors who are familiar with sexual harassment. The "Useful Addresses and Internet Sites" section at the back of this book lists some helpful groups.

To find the EEOC office nearest you, call:

1-800-669-4000

9to5, the National Association of Working Women, has a national hotline that handles work-related sexual harassment cases. You can reach 9to5 at:

1-800-522-0925

6. File an official complaint.

Sometimes people who have been severely harassed decide to take a serious step. Where you file a claim depends on where you were harassed.

If you were harassed at school, contact the U.S. Department of Education's Office for Civil Rights. Students must file claims within 180 days of the last incident of harassment. The office usually decides cases within three months. Also contact your state's education agency.

If you were harassed at work, contact the EEOC. Every state has an EEOC branch. Some states require that victims first file a claim with a state agency such as a human rights department. Then that agency can file with the EEOC. The length of time to file with the EEOC can vary, depending on state laws.

It is a good idea to talk with a job counselor or lawyer who is familiar with sexual harassment laws. That person can advise you about your options if you are considering filing a complaint or lawsuit. The EEOC and some women's groups have many people who can give you more detailed information. Check the back of this book for more contacts.

7. Go to court.

Some victims choose to go to court to stop their harassers. Going to court often takes great effort, a long time, and sometimes, a lot of money. Before you decide to go to court, you need to consider carefully how much effort you are willing to give your sexual harassment case. Courts can help victims, but going to court can take a toll emotionally and financially.

Points to Consider

What would you do if another student harassed you?

What would you do if an adult harassed you?

Why do you think it is important to keep track of harassment?

If your school has a sexual harassment policy, is it posted where students, teachers, and others can see it?

Chapter Overview

You are not responsible for being sexually harassed.

Sexual harassment is illegal.

You can act to protect yourself against sexual harassment.

Other people can help you defend yourself against sexual harassment.

Chapter 7

Important Stuff to Remember

Sexual harassment can make people feel bad. It is important to remember that sexual harassment is never your fault. However, you can do something to stop it. Here are some points to keep in mind about sexual harassment.

1. You are not responsible for being sexually harassed.
Sexual harassment happens to all kinds of people. It is a myth that only people who "ask for it" are harassed. You are not to blame if you are sexually harassed. Only harassers are responsible for their words and actions. Victims are never responsible for what harassers do or say.

2. Sexual harassment is illegal.

Sexual harassment is against the law in both Canada and the United States. It is prejudice based on sex. The law requires businesses to provide a workplace for their employees that is free from sexual harassment. Schools must do the same for students. Courts can fine not only the harassers but also schools or businesses that do not stop harassment.

3. You can act to protect yourself.

You cannot always stop sexual harassment before it happens, but you can do something. You can tell the harasser directly or in a letter that his or her behavior offends you. If you must, you can file a complaint or lawsuit to stop the harasser.

4. Other people can help you.

Many people are experienced in helping victims of sexual harassment. The back of this book lists some organizations concerned with sexual harassment. Groups such as 9to5, the National Association of Working Women, have tracked sexual harassment issues for years. Those groups can help victims stop harassment.

Points to Consider

Why do you think people who know the law and policies about sexual harassment still harass others?

How strong do you think the punishment should be for people who sexually harass others?

What more would you suggest the government, schools, or employers do to stop sexual harassment?

If you could form an organization to stop sexual harassment, what would it be like?

Glossary

civil rights (SIV-il RITES)—basic rights that all people have as citizens

Equal Employment Opportunity Commission (EEOC) (EE-kwul em-PLOI-muhnt op-ur-TOO-nuh-tee kuh-MISH-uhn)—the U.S. government agency created to deal with workplace discrimination, including sexual harassment

grievance (GREE-vuhnss)—a cause of distress that makes a person feel the need to complain; one way to stop sexual harassment is to file a grievance.

harass (huh-RASS)—to bother, disturb, or upset another person

harasser (huh-RASS-er)—a person who treats one or more persons meanly

harassment (ha-RASS-muhnt)—the act of disturbing, distressing, or hassling another person

hostile (HOSS-tuhl)—intended to hurt or be unfriendly or cruel

policy (POL-uh-see)—a written plan that helps people handle a situation; many companies and schools have sexual harassment policies.

rape (RAYP)—sex that is forced on someone; some cases of sexual harassment can lead to rape.

retaliation (ri-TAL-ee-AY-shuhn)—the act of doing something unpleasant or cruel to someone who has done the same to you

sexual harassment (SEK-shoo-wuhl ha-RASS-muhnt)—any unwelcome actions, words, or behaviors of a sexual nature

stereotype (STER-ee-oh-tipe)—an overly simple picture or opinion of a person, group, or thing

For More Information

Bouchard, Elizabeth. *Everything You Need to Know About Sexual Harassment.* New York: Rosen, 1997.

Chaiet, Donna, and Francine Russell. *The Safe Zone: A Kid's Guide to Personal Safety.* New York: William Morrow, 1998.

Gay, Kathlyn. *Rights and Respect: What You Need to Know About Gender Bias and Sexual Harassment.* Brookfield, CT: Millbrook, 1995.

Guernsey, JoAnn Bren. *Sexual Harassment: A Question of Power.* Minneapolis: Lerner, 1995.

Landau, Elaine. *Your Legal Rights: From Custody Battles to School Searches, the Headline-Making Cases That Affect Your Life.* New York: Walker, 1995.

Useful Addresses and Internet Sites

Canadian Human Rights Commission
Place de Ville, Tower A, #1300
320 Queen Street
Ottawa, ON KIA IEI
CANADA

Center for Individual Rights
1233 20th Street NW, Suite 300
Washington, DC 20036
www.wdn.com/cir/sh.htm

Prepare, Inc. (Protection, Awareness, Response
and Empowerment)
147 West 25th Street, 8th Floor
New York, NY 10001
1-800-345-KICK (5425)
www.prepareinc.com

U.S. Equal Employment Opportunity
Commission
1801 L Street NW
Washington, DC 20507
1-800-669-4000
www.eeoc.gov

Women's Legal Defense Fund
1875 Connecticut Avenue NW, Suite 710
Washington, DC 20009

Kids Help Hotline in Canada
kidshelp.sympatico.ca/help/index.htm
Information and tips on friendship, abuse,
sexual violence, and more

National Network for Youth
www.nn4youth.org
Adolescent abuse issues

Boys Town National Hotline
1-800-448-3000

Equal Rights Advocates
1-800-839-4372

Index

Index continued